INTO THE CONTINENT

ᐅᏁᏏ

OSKANA POETRY & POETICS

Emily McGiffin

Into the Continent

University of Regina Press

Printed and bound in Canada. The text of this book is printed on 100% post-consumer recycled paper with earth-friendly vegetable-based inks.

Cover art: "Rifle with Bayonet on a White Background" by Deana Robova / iStockphoto, and "Big Old Axe Isolated on White" by vav63 / iStockphoto

Cover design: Duncan Campbell, University of Regina Press

Interior layout design: John van der Woude, JVDW Designs

Series Editor: Randy Lundy
Managing Editor: Shannon Parr
Proofreader: Shannon Parr

The text and titling faces are Arno, designed by Robert Slimbach.

Canada Council   Conseil des arts
for the Arts   du Canada

Canadä

creative
SASKATCHEWAN

Library and Archives Canada Cataloguing in Publication

Title: Into the continent / Emily McGiffin.

Names: McGiffin, Emily, author.

Series: Oskana poetry & poetics ; 18.

Description: Series statement: Oskana poetry & poetics ; 18 | Poems. | Text printed in tête-bêche format.

Identifiers: Canadiana (print) 20230557589 | Canadiana (ebook) 20230557597 | ISBN 9780889779891 (softcover) | ISBN 9780889779907 (PDF) | ISBN 9780889779914 (EPUB)

Subjects: LCGFT: Poetry.

Classification: LCC PS8625.G52 I58 2024 | DDC C811/.6—dc23

10   9   8   7   6   5   4   3   2   1

UNIVERSITY OF REGINA PRESS
University of Regina
Regina, Saskatchewan
Canada S4S 0A2
TELEPHONE: (306) 585-4758
FAX: (306) 585-4699
WEB: www.uofrpress.ca
EMAIL: uofrpress@uregina.ca

We acknowledge the support of the Canada Council for the Arts for our publishing program. We acknowledge the financial support of the Government of Canada. / Nous reconnaissons l'appui financier du gouvernement du Canada. This publication was made possible with support from Creative Saskatchewan's Book Publishing Production Grant Program.

ACKNOWLEDGEMENTS

Much of this book was written during residencies at the Al Purdy
A-frame in Ameliasburgh, Ontario; Joya: arte + ecología in Spain; and
Cove Park in Scotland. Many thanks to the people who have given so
much of their time and energy to these magical places, in particular
Jean Baird, Eurithe Purdy, and Simon and Donna Beckman. I am
grateful to the Canada Council for the Arts and the Ontario Arts
Council for their financial support. I collected much of the material
for this book during my doctoral research at York University and
Rhodes University in South Africa and owe much to the generous
guidance of Cate Sandilands and Thembela Kepe, and to the
assistance of staff at the Amazwi South African Museum of Literature
and the Cory Library in Makhanda. The financial support of the
Social Sciences and Humanities Research Council of Canada and
York University made this initial research possible, and a fellowship at
the Institute for Advanced Studies in the Humanities at the University
of Edinburgh enabled further research and editing. Special thanks
are due to Amy Brant, former Research Manager for the Mohawks of
the Bay of Quinte at Tyendinaga, and her successor, Steven Lindsay-
Maracle. During my visit to Tyendinaga in 2018, Amy took the time
to explain the history of the Upper Mohawk Tract. Steven Lindsay-
Maracle offered comments on a final draft of the manuscript. Excerpts
of the text have appeared in *Northword Magazine* and *Hamilton Arts
& Letters*; thanks, Alec Follett and Matt Simmons, for your support
of my work. I submitted parts of this manuscript to awards that
it didn't win and journals who didn't publish it; thank you to the
juries, editors, and organizers for the time you spent reading the
work and for your dedication to literature. Thank you to the team at
University of Regina Press and the Oskana Poetry series, especially
Randy Lundy, Shannon Parr, and Karen Clark. Abundant gratitude
to Jan Zwicky, Dan Wylie, Fabienne Calvert Filteau, and Laurie D.
Graham for your thoughtful comments on earlier drafts and your
encouragement for the project. Finally, all my love to the home team
for your good company and good cheer on our journey together.

All their villages were destroyed and burnt,
all their fields turned into pasturage.

—Karl Marx on the Sutherland Clearances
Capital, Volume 1, Chapter 27

we carried endings with us | wreckage of the morning, detritus of all coal-hearted and eclipsing anguish of the now-divided life | there was the life before and now life after | life in the stink of smokestacks, drift of now-dissolving creatures of the tide | life overhung by the unspoken past and how things have unfurled | we hung the sails of our slave ships bared the land for cattle and for corn fenced and spliced it | onslaught of the sea and all the landscapes of our memories awash transformed | take now, the hurled curse, the lands of nakedness and mud, such things were done, unspeakable wrought handily and stitched upheaved from useless utterance of twilight's beauty | sickened inexcusable our vastness and excess what we hauled out what laid waste such thievery our souls their flesh the generous makings of their hands undone nothing could be righted nor repaired no degree of regret or contrition just extracted endless peeling back of skirts o how! too much of kicking out beneath you! what harrowed blight of whom bound and staked slash clothes bend flesh and pin and rend it leave perdition's fury in what proportion written out?

in what proportion dreaming

long hours on the tenuous and simple tracks appearing and receding in the ling | our feet in heathered depths expanses undertaken fleetly | all greenery bestowed the hilltops overburdened blooms and handholds in the flowered nooks, what truer kindnesses what openings and softnesses what tender whispers trail

then down the glade and trembling the tall grey-fluted sky
a goshawk wheels and here that inkling of the preyed-upon
and how, drifting up, flanked morning upon wing lifting
then spear, snatch passerine in razored grip and in the strath
blackhouses burn two hundred | circling, light falters, winks,
strikes raptor's wings and curled smoke

        unwanted here, the manufactured poor

cast backward glances at the soil of nativity
liveliest fields laid waste

sedge tuffets in the meadows, bellicose gorse

the beith the tawny owl the lark

companions of those long-dead jawbones
calling us and calling from the ground

sedges by a meadow blown softly
tipped with winter while grasses punch up sharp and green

mud banks stand bleak along the firth, glazed with tide
and between them skiffs at anchor

twisted wrack at watermark, mats and nests that insects leap from
flies circle, land, spin off

glens desolate and on the firth those sent to fish stand ankle
deep in muck while stormlight's bleak topography drives
breakers deathly through the curtained sleet and buckling
down they grip their pails, spade for clams

no thought of leaving : leaving came for us : hog-tied us
made us bilge water

worthless where we were
stones cast from fields | stones for ballast

marram thatch still crackles in the ears

charred timbers dropping
cottages smashed up to fence the cheviots

jetty and its masts a thistle, lines that web a forest
hull black and gleaming gilded, amphitrite at the bow

naval and merchant vessels jostle at the docks, masts sway
and in the bay fishing boats, barges, ferries with their tarred and
    weedy hulls

cormorants embrace the scene and ducks drift idle on the tide
dusk sidles in, port lights wink and shimmer on the bay

and here the ship, built for human cargo

involuntary cargo : draft : bulk exports

pelagic, i await my carriage

age-old green sea
its wavelets twist, flashing
as dark ghosts puff a sudden cold

gulls, kittiwakes
keen above the slick mud
bobbing blunt fishing boats and men

haul in the creels
their flopping silver cargo
their scuttling crabs and kelp gatherers

sling tangled weed
slick and stinking below
rippled purple hills that draw back

abandoned
a sickening spillage
the ship keeling in the wind

in water's
hands now, age-old
murderous sea; all morning

home recedes
highlands flatten
to cuneiform waves that smack

the hull a rising
reek as cargo vomits
steeling through another dark

passage, canal
to an arena where we emerge
gladiators, bestiarii, trench-diggers of history

vessel piloted through squalls by mappa mundi of unspoiled
treasure, of countries lecherous for cast-iron men with sheep,
countries to explore and quarry, catalogue and overhaul
heroic sunsets smoulder, strengthen, glow and
afterglow, violet scaling up the wall behind the clouds that
flame the water bloodshot pearl grey, the ship cacophony
of crew and galling cargo grunting hogs and hens sails that
belly out and snap

old lives stillborn
our burial at sea

dreaming to the wakeful shout, the palaver
that heaves me out of slumber's skin while water
sluices past the hull, ear pressed close
to planks' and rigging's groan, the night watch
bangs about, in interminable night, translucent
creatures drift phosphoric, constellated
each watery note that hooks me fishlike strands me
in the clammy bunk, where ebbing i contain
my drowning voice

what thrust open and shadowing the golden of a fleetest tide?
    arrival
is a perilous grey and slapdash shallows break
upon the gunwales, keel burnishes the reef and dips | a tender
lapstrake ferrying the banished through this stricken league of tide
awash and buckling | each purple-turbaned snail drags a hind foot
rockward dash of spume engulfs all pools of sinewed blistered
weed and cresting now the froth licks under air freighted
with the heavy damp, that sweet and cloying scent of fish
    and twisted wrack
gulls clamouring the whistle and the grunt
of oarlocks feather dip and draw | opening and fanning sea-soft
    flowers
in their pools take my fingers kiss them, lurching
hermits in their whelkish homes sidle curious
then smashing how the waves blast in! toss sand toss weed
toss splintered elementary flash | kelp too, serpentine
and lashed splotched corraline and nodding
how the salt tide heaves and thrusts | hauling
from the shallows wetly glistening we emerge on foreign shore

then tentative then cryptic then fleeting
salt sky pillowy alabaster | unremarkable
the furrowed sunset, estranged
nighted kingdoms of beetle, insectivore,
jackal, churlish toad | heckling and mighty
the night demons, the peevish, lilting sickle
of a variegated moon

trudging difficult through pig-iron dawn
we carry means without an end

                              torturous dreaming
                                  lean undone

vulture winging slow and high
sky scorched white and lone bird
scything under fisted bright:

                      fiery

               insistent as a heart

          high-minded as a magistrate

          heavy as the tablet whereon
            all sacraments are writ

on
and on into the continent
glassy pan of sand and scrub marching on ahead

castaways, dispatched to master
                                    a thorned land
                                blitzed and running
                        tearing off in hands-up flight

home no house but mud bricks crumbling
crooked door jamb termite-gouged

yellowwood black-throated, twisted
bears the smoke-dark reedy ceiling
vermin shuffling about

house no home but indigent bricks
strange man and stranger still the servant
woman in a bullock skin, his prisoner

i climb the hill behind the shanty
heat drags slick fingers down my ribs
thorny scrub—puir, dun—
staggers to the line of empty hills

a dirty plague of sheep
paws at the ground, imploring
grass to issue from the dust

now thorny twigs and all the heartsickness that settles with the grime | ivory blades of scarified noon fall daily | whereupon I wring my hands and pace half-blinded with each homeward thought unbuttoned, knifed | whereupon each daybreak boulders, millstones, airless trunks of earth arrive to press and suffocate | awake to dim light with strange birds already crying through it | dawn breaks on thorn trees gaunt with desiccating heat

no end to it, the smelter, fires i am
      strung up by my heels, nightly pinned and excavated   eaten!
by a great fish with its needle-toothed   mouth   prisoner of my ribs'
      cage anthill and termite-mound devoured, collapsing!

in this desert no river to efface me

he wants to carve his way upriver but there is no river just parched gravel where water ought to flow and so he grapples, grasping and determined, slippery with effort, to press my limbs into the sheepskins as he makes his bloody way through thorns and biting insects, cobras, lions, everything that wants him gone but bayonet raised he fights hard into his continent and gains the pinnacle he strives for, plants his flagstaff, spreads his pestilence of seed and shudders with the thrill of it, rolls his slick mass and snores contented in the cricket air while wakeful in his murky pool, a fish that's not yet drowned, i think of hook and knife and razor, all easy ends to share

a mantis crouches near the sooty timbers, elbows crooked, paws
turned under at the wrist | it watches me with generous eyes
where does it find such devotion? what hopes grow in its tiny
    flowered heart?
locusts bound into the drying maize and sun arrives, alighting
on the bowed leaves, smoke curling as the cooking fire grips
what is it to remember? blurred endings and beginnings, sun
rising to its zenith only to fall | to speak of god and duty
the bible is the size and weight of one man's hand

such is loss of home and family, of gladness for the string
of days before me | i could dream of the household i was
bound for, its comforts and joys, its lynchpins of man and
wife, honest work and idle hours, earned rest of age, shadows
of our backlit selves stretched forth entwined with swallows
fleetest in the violet morning, looping through the air

life crumbles out of youth
when heat was done came frost

you! withering fiend of half-demented devil! what frogspawn, what vile excrement of forgotten, mangy dogs | i conjure all evil, my eyes spit curse and lightning, my hands flay quivering each muscle from the ribs | what strength in these my hands! enough to pull down rock face and the blue that holds it | my bristling hands the thorny hills the quick-forgotten thunder is my breath | what heart upbraided what petty desirings of certitude and soft | nought but conquest militarily your project your minion i stitching daily the raiments of power and what thought of possession? not my skin but yours ruled by bible fist and buckled length of leather

the man has gone
called by his superiors
to advance the east frontier

to sever bonds of blood and kinship forged
over one hundred generations

battened to the ground
a lineage, a firmament
the earth the bones the breath

now i languish with a servant
trapped by war and emptied land
by sheep pleading desolate
for a swoop of muir lodged in blood

memory | sometimes in the afternoon
thoughts swing on a lunge from stabled gloom beyond
the wall of desert to soft ground under hooves, heathered air
i conjure from the white-tusked scrub
yellow flowered, queuing leaves

this desert stretch all wind and silence
but for voices of the blue cranes dancing
raised wings and slender throats, they lift, subside

grief trails me like a broken wing

one day you have a home, a trade
the next you find yourself aboard a ship

displaced by sheep, burdened
with sheep, tasked

with subsequent displacement, armed
to the teeth to uphold the holy struggle

the proud-backed woman nancy
imprisoned for her trespasses

muscles through our toil
of living on this land so freshly

civilized and how pale
by comparison i find myself

quiet drifted in and settled with the blown grit
just the sound of nancy
grinding at the quern

her shadow in the doorway

she'd passed her hands over
the dark marks on my throat
welts we each bore

regarding me with averted eyes

absent characters in the epics of men's telling
accessories to stories of his valour,
heroic conquest of a hostile land

did i exist
before this moment of arrival
that second birth on scoured shore
the spume erased my tracks

is there freedom in a voice?
or is it made for speaking only
happy paeans to the nation

i would have gone on saying nothing
no words fitting
land's open-throated silence

but for nancy's quiet clicks

we watched each other
with dead commiseration
each so much less a citizen

amid the dingy rags and sheepskins,
gazing through a cleft of brightness in the mud-brick wall
faded, threadbare land and ochre,

sheep panted lying in the heat and kiltered
light skulked amid the dust motes
and the aloes bloomed, torches blazing on the hills
what were the odds of death from such confinement?

let me tell you of the quaggas that gathered to sip at the dam
they stood beneath the thorn trees, streaked with light and shade
at dusk, the gaunt euphorbia, scrubby
spekboom lay shadows on the yard, then stars streamed thick
as cream ladled on the indigo, the scent of renosterbos caught
in hot, sweet air, and up the hillsides bitter aloes stood regal,
waiting, bearing hearts of flame

in the moonlight nancy
staved off my fevered death

whisper of a kettle
her strong efficient hands

if god is to be found
it's in such hearts as hers

the finest pain and bright of it
seated at the apex of the sky, the throbbing and all-seeing eye floods
false water on the land

still, scorching air and under it the ground is glossed with truth | heat knocks against the roof, against sweat, mine, and blood of someone else, the mewling stranger cradled from its housing, slick lump in the dawning hours | it is abraham, adam, jude he has no name but shouts them all from warming bellows he will use to forge himself richard, henry, george he is all names and none, the pure and nameless life that kicked me, that heard hoof beats of the distant eland and hastened to join their feet, measuring his stride across the plains, crushing the spiders and the antlions beneath them he who will claim the veld and master it, what single name could i bestow?

his arrival is the wind stealing up, the rushing wind that
bends all things beneath it, its hollow voice lifts clothes that
stood calm in the heat, that spirits up the dust that douses
us | on and on he shouts his name and his name is molten
glass and leaded | where is family? why have you brought
me here?

he lies in nancy's arms

nancy who swaddles him who shushes his cries
nancy who whispers the first human words

what does she tell him?

she stands beneath the lintel, between me and flaming death,
turns his little head toward the oceanic land that walks on
without an end, the sun ablaze, the bustards watching

his father out there, laying claim to the horizon

in the country of her arms lies
a pink and bleating soldier's son
called to father what will follow

all the long thereafter fever scorches, floods

let me tell you of the instances of perplexing beauty
brown arms in firelight the winter's only warmth the child
held between us perhaps his future would be shaped instead
by what we taught, the gentleness he learned
those months before the war returned

let me tell you of the loveliness,
a sky of bright and blazing blue, wind singing
out across the boundless earth,
goading steenboks to a canter
across the near hills prickly with green,
the ground all sage and dun, and farther, soft
with distance the rippled violet range

trundling
the length of days the tumble bugs
hoard their aliquot of time

if it were so if it were merely
a blessing visited upon us
small miracle of unknown
origin destiny duration
then what need had we
of anything but sun and grain
the pane of rain gathering
behind the dam
the scent of earth and skin
gentle as those cattle freed
to follow inclination

throw open the door, let the wind come in
let it shift the quiet that has gathered

what happens in the desert? on the frontier?
those places where humanity forgets itself

i have not seen i know
the returning soldier tells me

with his hands, his heft, the nature
of the tactics that they practiced

dead thump of war comes home
another clearance

men clamour for more
land on which to propagate their sheep

a boundary drawn redrawn as utility dictates
demarcating the desired

and undesirables: the labouring class
the lazy poor, idle vagrants, primitive gaels

the natives, no longer bronze, noble
are cunning now and filthy

not too dirty to leave a mark upon

nancy purple around the eyes
and golden amidships, plum

claims staked everywhere

or wily theft
we choose our allegiances

my body an ark
carrying successors like a chambered nautilus

what i was placed here to do
ferry the unborn
across the inhospitable land
make a bed amid the thornbush
make a tea table, forge the domestic
bliss of my country
raise them as heirs
draw our lineage in the sand

all to say that endings were required

i dug and dragged
the soil on an ox hide

mounded it and placed the rocks
a rampart staunched the red earth's trickle

our home—this country—has no room
for brothers of such kind

you will ask what i oversaw
what kinships or betrayals

trifles among the larger tasks
of placing animals on this unpeopled terrain
with long arms, with words like "cluck" and "wool"

of ordering new classes: as we had served
we now possessed
and so war blooms here

and on the frontier
a resolute flower
its season come round again

beneath the weight of rain the earthwork crumples
water awakes to its new life

tears through the breach to forge a path
across the desert like a cobra gleaming

a flicker of recoiling scales
then its memory a whisper on my hands

who are we in its absence?

INTO THE CONTINENT

ᐃᓄᑲ

OSKANA POETRY & POETICS

Into the Continent

Emily McGiffin

University of Regina Press

ᐅᓇᐳ

OSKANA POETRY & POETICS
BOOK SERIES

Publishing new and established authors, Oskana Poetry
& Poetics offers both contemporary poetry at its best
and probing discussions of poetry's cultural role.

Randy Lundy—*Series Editor*

Advisory Board

Sherwin Bitsui	Tim Lilburn
Robert Bringhurst	Duane Niatum
Laurie D. Graham	Gary Snyder
Louise Bernice Halfe	Karen Solie

PREVIOUS BOOKS IN THE SERIES:

Measures of Astonishment: Poets on Poetry,
presented by the League of Canadian Poets (2016)

The Long Walk, by Jan Zwicky (2016)

Cloud Physics, by Karen Enns (2017)

The House of Charlemagne, by Tim Lilburn (2018)

Blackbird Song, by Randy Lundy (2018)

Forty-One Pages: On Poetry, Language and Wilderness,
by John Steffler (2019)

Live Ones, by Sadie McCarney (2019)

Field Notes for the Self, by Randy Lundy (2020)

Burden, by Douglas Burnet Smith (2020)

Red Obsidian, by Stephan Torre (2021)

Pitchblende, by Elise Marcella Godfrey (2021)

Shifting Baseline Syndrome, by Aaron Kreuter (2022)

Synaptic, by Alison Calder (2022)

The History Forest, by Michael Trussler (2022)

Dislocations, by Karen Enns (2023)

Wrack Line, by M.W. Jaeggle (2023)

Emily McGiffin was born on
Tla-o-qui-aht territory and raised on the
lands of the Ts'uubaa-asatx and Quw'utsun
Nations. She is currently a Research
Fellow at University College London.

But in fact, it is capitalist accumulation itself that constantly produces...a population which is superfluous to capital's average requirements for its own valorization, and is therefore a surplus population.

—Karl Marx on the production of an industrial reserve army
  Capital, Volume 1, Chapter 25

We were a company of the rejected; the drunken, the incompetent, the weak, the prodigal, all who had been unable to prevail against circumstances in the one land, were now fleeing pitifully to another; and although one or two might succeed, all had already failed.

—Robert Louis Stevenson, *From the Clyde to California*

in what proportion evidence

in what proportion mere belief?

the end has come and gone already, charred apocalypse of
steel, cotton, mute legions of the midnight shifts pigstick the
heaths beyond carbuncle mills, their galling notes of perjury
darken the lacklustre morn | taken to extremes and flogged,
the moorlands overturn and heave; they arch their broke,
despoiled backs, flayed thickets given up for rows of sooty
brick | in these excesses, church bells and nine thousand
voices raised in mourning strain, their canticles of praise
and suffering fitted to the afternoon | what animals there
were have gone, fled the utterance, fled damnable pistons,
engines, blades, smooth-talking mathematics | brushstrokes
falling off the canvas, slumber shudder through the dreams
of whiskers, paws and antlers, furred sorrow of retreat | what
place for us in these new machinations of a nation's wealth?
o empire!

our animated souls alone and shadowed, our hands
bereft of soil, hearts of titillated dawn

what beginnings? even the quern
work of my grandmother's hands
outlawed smashed

heaved into the loch

so magnus carried corn
· to the laird's mill grubbed up
specie to bring home the meal

then down the weald and flickering the gone archdeacon
sky, the ruddy hawk spins upwards, that inkling of the
preyed-upon and how, drifts up, flanked morning upon
wing pillowing then lance down, snatch ribbon in a razored
grip | feathers plume a raptor's leg, a horse's tethered to a
barge, willowy in the tailwind drifting | yes, they drew the
lines and cut it up, open fields and the moors | circling,
light falters, winks, strikes raptor's wings and then the
crops | now turnpikes, now cotton, now freewheeling
toffs, now things set unravelling, elaborately planned, land
management in bureaus, twisting reason striving past the
undercut and robbed

put plainly, father's house in brutish flame collapses,
    shelter buckles, crackles, timbers lancing down
outside, blue-pencilled pastures   outside,
they hash the commons by parliamentary decree

                                    vagrants trundled off
                              are there no workhouses?

air stained with autumn and the white frosts crizzle
pippin windfalls
soften to the ground

in the strait tidewater courses past
bending weeds that furl amid the rocks, starlight
gurgles in the throat

no end to leaving, fluid
limitless and cold

my end arrives, ordeal by water

long dun symmetry of manor house on clyde, calm grace of
tall and even windows, rows of chimney pots | gulls call and
wheel over poplars, river

apple blossoms luminous at dusk as gathered stars | a
golden swath of fading daffodils | opal water that spring's
wind kneels to lap

and the ship glides on toward the sea, moon
                                        rising, moon
                    buoyed by its own surety, fat and rich

medusa sidelong in the current trailing streamers,
      murky, phantom
and pelagic, blind and mute and without will

                         like a common weed
                         the sea-swell takes us

churn and heft and thrust of it
brine sloshing in the hatches swilling blur of heaved and
sickly-sweet nine gallons brandy drenched and overhauled
a steerage cargo barely human grunting sniffling muffled
coughs and cries festering with cholera diphtheria fevers
scarlet typhoid yellow amid rats and bilious air and one by
one we bury children in the waves

and on the air, as if a rime of salt,
dim outlines of some childish drawing,
memories of this place imagined, a city's ghost
on shorelines empty but for driftwood, pines,
and then white houses, strung
like sheets pegged up to dry

arrival is a knife pulled through a fruity rind, bright flesh
laid open on the ground to coax the birds
birds descending from the heavens, beauty
threaded through their mouths and lungs,
birds my plumed companions
in a solitary flight

a clamour at the dock and no familiar face
the passengers disperse
no one arrives for me

                              and now? i pay a coin
for the transport of my trunk, the sky low, air thick, damp
streets slick with mud and hawking throngs

                         the weeks roll by, no word

                         i beg lodging in a stable
                         i do washing for my keep
                         hauling water from the lake
                         knuckles raw and bleeding

i ask authorities in kingston
who tell me *place an advert*
list names and meeting place
this sort of thing has grown all too common

               he may have gone to york, niagara, cornwall
                 he may have bought a farm somewhere

                         and changed his name
                         and found another wife

unstoppering his rye he eyes me up and down and midriff
swigging
gaze cutting me to squares

a home for you, he promises and winks

                                        my countryman
                he sees the ailments of history lodged in me

ignorant of my ignorance, innocent
of innocence] adder with its patterned back, its diamond
coiled strike hair crumpled in your hand cast iron
slash and bloody forehead cheekbone crumpled mouth] blunt fist
of clenching hurt misshapen ball this waspish fury wrenched distorted
all tongues of sweet delight and dawn of angled gold abundance
grimace now, annihilated] now muck and blast and pestilence
] now abscesses of sorrowed wrath]
i who had seen apple blossoms beaded with the dewy morn
and purplish dawn with scent of lilacs streaming and longed only
for such golden for small new green for kittens undrowned
for bountiful and pleasant fields softly hilled and sea foam things
you disdain and trample
reforging as your tempered calloused twin] here: slag
piles] here: mountains scalped for coal] here: no dreaming
left no hope for loveliness] all fouled and piteous fancy
snarled] and funk-addled
trash piles and wounded dogs and paupers dragging cursed
filthy bodies through the streets] everywhere riled blistered,
thrashed and overcome] nightly pain sewering in runnels to slotted
obsolete imaginings] ah! ideas pinioned
mired before their flight] all things we might have been before this
otherwise]
before we'd learned to do such things] before
the ship and fire the fences] before the possible snuffed out

a landless drunkard deep in debt, a thief

that's the succour that god sent

arriving on the upper mohawk tract
we build the shanty though we have no title

or title is official whim

we live by poaching timber
their petitions to the Crown dismissed

we occupy the granted lands, we open them

haul each massive trunk with piebald oxen
skidding it across the snow

in the widening clearing we sow cabbages

the squat shanty darkens with soot and grime
nights, whiskey and the sting of leather

and nightly champion cries from anguished yearnings
auger, little screw shank, turning on itself and driving in

when it ends, i slide outside to wash out what i can,
    summer night alive
with insects, stars, bats dipping
                wind sighs through the reigning vegetation

i press the burns that fester on my arms
go! take your implement to the oxen   go sate yourself
    with sheep

we flayed the land and set about
reorganizing, resourceful
as enlightenment, as a nation

              the plants i could not coax from gravelled soil
                      stood mesmerized by frost
              gnawed by insects, turned to stubble by the deer
                      all we have are crookhorn peas
                      i crouched threshing in the yard

sumac clotted at the forest edge
marsh a burnished copper

how brief the glorious leaves
golden as cathedral windows

now their carpet thickens on the ground
rustling underfoot and overhead the blackbird

sleek and dark amid the thousand shades of gold
it cackles under thinning panes of sun

overhead the forest murmurs to itself
green steps from slender grasses through the shrubbery to
saplings overhead, the ceiling of stained green and scarlet-gold
skyward the yellow trees
whisper bleak secrets

we fell one trunk and then another, clearing
out this state of nature, quelling
sylvan gloom to glades white
with sunlight, providence
blest the struggle

each massive trunk takes ten days to haul out
he says, and fetches just a tanner

he comes back reeking, proclamations slurred

ringed by thickset walls of filthy trunks
i brace my unit of exchange

this curled opening of air and light amid the nighted trees,
    this sphere
a prison, suffocating, that hems in, oppresses with its gloom,
with threats, dark haunts of wild cats and wolves

axing out the trees, we turned the forest to white spaces
when winter fell, opened lakes of snow
we put our labour on the land, made wilderness, removed it
laid snake fences that declared it ours

alone, illegal, we lived like families of the drowned
weighted with our cold remembrances

now leafless twigs and all the heartsickness that settles with the snow and lowering winter sky | whereupon I wring my hands and pace half-blinded with each homeward thought an open wound | whereupon with each daybreak, boulders, millstones, airless trunks of earth arrive to press and suffocate | awake to gunmetal dawn warming on the silent trees, white and gaunt with hoar

at times on the path beyond our clearing
people from the lakeside passed amid the trees

hunting or travelling or spying
on our progress we didn't know or care

we ran for the long arm
firing into the air into the space

where they had stood waiting
to burn us out disgorge us

as we slept wreak a thousand horrors
on our naked unimpeachable flesh

beneath frills of ice the creek flows silver
over petty stones and scours merrily

brightening the morning, that rush of cold
and clenched within my fists the braided
handle of a pail

somewhere far beyond the trees
life is carefree, garlanded
the officers feast

and the infantry drag ourselves frostbitten
through snowbanks beyond enemy lines

god writes history while men make war
on the civilians what sense is there
in anger but thinking of their thick

and fleshy necks, i tip the pail of shit
and watch it spill into the creek

the boy was born into snow
born like the snow, like the memory of it or
its loss of memory its enveloping drifts its gift

snow mounding, drifting over me forgotten
on this far edge of the still-treed world, trees
on all sides, supple spirits, leaning on the sky

snow and then the hoar that clasps it, fractal,
winking from each twig, lit cold gracing the air

the boy who is all things to me now, all of home, all of family
he who contains the lineage in his pink and wrinkled skin,
in this swaddled assemblage of his limbs, a monarch alight
in a downing rain

crouched alone i tend the embers of a generation, the man
gone to peddle timber that will raise it

undivided weight of mourning looms nothing here to eat but pigweed, sawdust | days move past in single file, stillborn life, stilted happiness undone the grief an ocean | o to sit lowly with the animals amid the stumps, turning in the sun to watch them graze, such hunger ache i'd thought was past | here the yard a quagmire strewn with kitchen scraps the chickens squabbling and reek of cow and pig, walls and ceiling caked with soot the mass of daily toil felling trees thick as three men hacking up the undergrowth heaving the ploughshare amid the stumps and knotted roots that split its wooden teeth | we will strive with numbing toil until the future has its fill of us

crouched behind the milk pail
the boy sees how it is done, how a man

grasps a woman's wrist behind her, lifts it
up her spine, how he grips

the hair mounded at the neck and shepherds
her to the table, plants her breast there, hoists

the skirts | cheek against the slats, she can press
her teeth together, blink her eyes at the depths

of passion a man holds for his possessions
arrayed around him in his house

he foists his rage on me

like a house on fire
throwing again, again
its flames into the world

he stands on the winning side
of loss, transmuting grief's
shackles, its propulsion

what the past built
what it took, what it gave
us to take freely

this inheritance unites us

walls of somber trees unending
death lurks under and amongst them

slumped in his chair the earnings
drain into his fetid skull

country of earnest cheerfulness, the steady
drip of destitution cuts

a hole through the close air
mired in the cruelty of squalor

the boy accepts what each day brings, fitting it silent into his chest

and in this way collects an understanding, growing quickly

guarded, jumpy, stoic—more like a body

sinking in a swamp, muck claiming by increments

the person who recedes into its icy depths

i wish the stones
had been more lasting

weighty, they should have moored us
to the ground that birthed them

but a stone house
becomes a stone fence

a field of sheep
a ship-loving landlord

great philanthropy

acre on acre of stumps and mud
crushed the moss-soft shadows, sparrows
harboured in the leaves

pilfering
we killed off gloom
laid barren dappled shadows

in the clearings
nothing spoke

we brought ends with us, carried like a torch

and now, trees greatly gone, light falls in cutting swaths

i left the smoky shanty and stepped amid the stumps | ten
years i have watched them rot the clearing pooling out
around us | he left three weeks ago to haul a log

taking the boy by his little hand i follow dim tracks dwindling
into the woods | does he lie injured in the snow? did he fall
ill somewhere and now lies sweating out a fever? did he
drop drunkenly through the ice and sink? die drunken in
a brawl? stabbed at cards when he was found a cheat? or
maybe drank and gambled all his earnings and, struck by
an uncommon pang of decency, was too ashamed to come
back empty-handed | perhaps he languishes in prison |
most likely he has tired of this life and disappeared into the
colony to try again; he sold his handsome pair of oxen, took
a steamship to niagara with earnings buried in the snow |
cold sparkles in the quiet air | the hungry child cries
                    deserted, there is no place for us but here

alone with the boy, oxen gone
sheep carried off by wolves, the birds return by increments

chattering their blessings to the greening oaks
cold eases back, retreating from the thawing soil

again i press the gathered seeds into the rooty loam amid the
    stumps
patternings of green around us, shifting, crowding out the sky

gloom goes on, and ague, and mildew,
creeping from the lighted angles, curtaining
disorder, putrid | underbrush unlovely, dank

shrill gnats prolific the sallow light
slumps underfoot in puddled moss, not yet
stippled into barley the simmering pines

where does the petering rain retreat to? blockish
clods and cumulus lifting from my mute blue labour,
forgery of signals, the puckish shift of cirrus, gnats
woebegone, a festering miasma at the marsh

hieroglyph inscriptions, birdfoot on sand | deer
trail ropish shadows from the disappearing sun

and even ordinary evening overtaken shadowy
long sliding falcon pocketed by woods
little stream slickens in its smooth, brown throat

what did it
] matter we would live our days in squalor or he would
    come, some man
or other finding cause to drag us from the land we squatted
    on as saplings
                            sprang around and thickened
in the waist we gave up beating
back the bush it was
relentless] bush itself
would drive us out if we weren't dragged

they didn't drag
     ]   merely arrived
shifty-eyed, dog-toothed, sat some hours in the corner with
    a flask

and fixative yellow not turning, how in lasting dapper green
he hews each pawed and tender thing and knifing now his
    rockdove
mind is kettling unrest——from the rubied fire he plucks an
    owl's talon

soft green shifts through its shades, yellow]
      called out by frost, the cedars flagging and the ash,
nuthatches roving down the trunks

now modest slender plants of all the
      ] all the heartsick pinnacles the longing and the death of
what we'd hoped, here, it goes greedily what lean tendrils of [
      of power root themselves in / fledgling morning unkempt]
      i lifting? i kneeling? cratered, i falling wrecked into the
      slim wastes of might,
      breath of
      power pushing where
      ] it wills each limb of
      of mine a sorrow, skin a sack of sad
my skin a sack that hopelessness made gaunt >\ what claim had i to
? i knocked back and]   [
wishing held me in

in murderous winter we slaughter
our last starved hen, unstring her pearly coil
of eggs, then learn again to live with hungry

boil bits of bark and twigs, chip
the frozen ground for acorns
whatever grubs might sleep there

the boy folds into an asterisk of bones
we grasp at sleep, the lone relief
from our immurement

now turning, now flaying triumphant
the long inkling of striated days, i dreamed
absent brothers, sisters, friends | honed
by wind and silence

despair a long accrual, dinginess of years
that pucker on the skin, time a hook
weighted, sinking, too perilous to hold

                   to watch a white moth stutter
                                      across the gap
between the shanty and the trees,
                   gold-dust hanging in the air around the cedars,
pine boughs dark, rain
                                      silvery upon them, geese
        clattering overhead and in the hearth,
                                      clack
and shift of charred and whitened branches,
                                      leaky shingles drip into the dirt

                   such elements make silence

        to be alone
                amid the sinking
                         dusk, to brood
        on one moth's long and solitary flight
                         through deathly snow, descending frost
toward some distant
                         unimaginable future

cold skin of the blue world unremitting
my words move under it and effervesce
they are a breath themselves that fill the air
rising to greet the wind and soundlessness
how mounting like smoke above the tent of trees
i sent them out to gaze where i could not, a safeguarding
my words a thrust of steel, a claymore
dashed against the reticent flesh or, if not,
a germ of plant expanding tentatively against its shell
then hastening, finding the enlarging taste of soil, air,
the bright expanse of space above it
and when asked, as if a sluice gate opened, a gear engaged,
yarn pulled from a skein, words come, tugged out
and being follows as of to remain, to leave
its traces, seeding this peopled soil
with ink smudges, fingerprints, epigraphs
of breath hung on the winter air

and as we sleep the peopled land unfurls
neighbours stepping in to right the winter's ills

they lift the latch and step in
lift us lousy from the grime,
the filth of our excrement and carry us

to the forest to be healed
we watch the trees flick past sliding
snowbound behind the muffled hoofbeats

the gleaming frozen ground
from the lake the village rises

we lie in the hut's warm quiet
in scents of burned herbs and hides
the boy sleeps quietly

                              and dusk falls
taking form from thickening air
wash by wash, inking over
the silhouetted spruce

spruce, white birches, charcoal sky
we are clean and fed
and the woods are beautiful

almost like a home

i move carefully amid the people,
clad in thickening forgetfulness

it serves me, amnesia
clenched like a bullet in the teeth

this morning my rattling cough
blooms scarlet

the land we lived on once
drawn up, quartered, sold

to men who can own it
its benevolent provision

we will make for the capital
for the edifices of the Crown

morning closed, snow sews the varied shades
to voicelessness and a ragged call tears through: lost
blackbird, shadow in the drifting flakes

i lift my hands into a triangle to watch its flight
from branch to twig, a shard of night that lifts
alights | life no flow but scattershot, a jetsam

without bearing as i walk into the snow